Rookie Read-About™ Science

It Could Still Be A Mammal

By Allan Fowler

Images supplied by VALAN Photos

Consultants:
Robert L. Hillerich, Ph.D., Bowling Green
State University, Bowling Green, Ohio

Mary Nalbandian, Director of Science,
Chicago Public Schools, Chicago, Illinois

Winnona Park
Elementary School

ℚ CHILDRENS PRESS ®
CHICAGO

Series cover and interior design by Sara Shelton

Library of Congress Cataloging-in-Publication Data

Fowler, Allan.
  It could still be a mammal / by Allan Fowler.
    p. cm.—(Rookie read-about science)
    Summary: Identifies the characteristics of mammals and provides
  specific examples including the whale, bat, kangaroo, and puppy.
    ISBN 0-516-04903-8
    1. Mammals—Juvenile. [1. Mammals.] I. Title.   II. Series.
  QL706.2.F69   1990   90-2161
  599—dc20   CIP
                                                             AC

  10 11 12 13 14 15 16 17 R 02 01

How do you know it's a mammal?

If it has a backbone,
and it has hair or fur,
and it is warm-blooded,
and the babies drink milk
from the mother's body—
it's a mammal!

Dogs are mammals.

Cows are mammals.

Horses are mammals, too.

But what if it looks like
a fish and lives in the
ocean? It could still be
a mammal

like a whale

or a dolphin.

What if it has flippers instead of legs? It could still be a mammal

like a sea lion

or a walrus.

What if it flies like a
bird? It could still be
a mammal

like a bat.

Pandas and bears and most other mammals are covered with hair or fur.

But this mammal is covered
with spines. It's a porcupine.

18

And this mammal, an armadillo, lives inside a hard shell.

A baby kangaroo stays
inside its mother's pouch.

A mammal could be as small as a mouse

or as big as an elephant,

as fat as a hippopotamus

or as tall as a giraffe.

It could be as playful as
a kitten

or as clever as a chimp.
It's still a mammal.

But do you know who is
the smartest mammal
in the world?

You are!

It's a fact—people are
mammals too!

Words You Know

It is a mammal.

It has a backbone.
It has hair or fur.
It is warm-blooded.
The babies drink milk from the mother's body.

armadillo

bat

bear

chimp

cow

dog

dolphin

elephant

giraffe

hippopotamus

horse

kangaroo

kitten

mouse

panda

porcupine

sea lion

walrus

whale

31

Index

About the Author

Allan Fowler is a free-lance writer with a background in advertising. Born in New York, he lives in Chicago now and enjoys traveling.

Photo Credits

© Valan—© Robert C. Simpson, Cover, 21, 30 (bottom right); © J. A. Wilkinson, 5, 29 (center right); © Val & Alan Wilkinson, 6, 29 (center left); © Michael J. Johnson, 7, 30 (center left); © Fred Bruemmer, 9, 13, 31 (center right & bottom); © Kennon Cooke, 10, 28 (top), 29 (bottom left); © S. J. Krasemann, 12, 23, 30 (top right), 31 (center left); © Wayne Lankinen, 15, 28 (bottom right); © Aubrey Lang, 16, 17, 29 (top left), 31 (top left); © Albert Kuhnigk, 18, 31 (top right); © Karl Weidmann, 19, 28 (bottom left); © John Cancalosi, 20, 30 (center right); © Arthur Christiansen, 22, 24, 29 (bottom right), 30 (top left); © Wouterloot-Gregoire, 25, 30 (bottom left); © Marguerite Servais, 26, 29 (top right)

COVER: Panda